Bishops' Conference of England & Wales

LIVING+SHARING
OUR FAITH

A NATIONAL PROJECT OF CATECHESIS
AND RELIGIOUS EDUCATION

Walking the Road

reflecting on the gospel story

Dympna Magee

Published with the authority of
Department for Catholic Education and Formation, Bishops' Conference of England and Wales

Collins

Collins Liturgical Publications
8 Grafton Street, London W1X 3LA

Collins Dove
PO Box 316, Blackburn, Victoria 3130
Collins Liturgical New Zealand
PO Box 1, Auckland

ISBN 0 00 599 262 1

First published 1990
© 1990 Department for Catholic Education and Formation
Bishops' Conference of England and Wales

Nihil obstat Fr Anton Cowan, *censor*

Imprimatur Rt. Rev. John Crowley V.G.
                    Bishop in Central London
Westminster, 5th July, 1990

Designed by Mary Lou Winters fsp

Photo credits   Cover: Mary Lou Winters fsp
                        All other photos Mary Lou Winters fsp
                        except the following:
                                    p.30 Vincent Lewis
                                    p. 83 J.L. Law
                                    p. 91 Lorenzo Lees

Manufactured in Great Britain by Hunter & Foulis, Edinburgh.

Acknowledgements

All Scripture texts from the Revised Standard Version, Catholic Edition, ©1966,
by Division of Christian Education of the National Council of Churches of
Christ in the United States of America, reprinted with permission; p.20:
Concerning the Divine Word, by St John of the Cross from **Poems of St John of
the Cross**, translated by Roy Campbell (*Collins Fount*); p.43: *A Drink of Water* by
Seamus Heaney, from **Field Work**, reprinted by permission of Faber and Faber
Ltd; p.62: *A Prayer to the Pain of Jesus* from **The Hour of the Unexpected** by
John Shea, ©1977, Tabor Publishing, a division of DLM, Inc., Allen, TX 75002;
p.67: *The Song of the Bread* by Huub Oosterhuis, from **Your Word is Near**
(*Newman Press*); p.74: *The Prodigal Son* by Elizabeth Jennings, from **Tributes**
(*Carcanet*), reprinted by permission; p.86: *Now the green blade riseth*, words by
JMC Crum from **The Oxford Book of Carols** (*OUP*), reprinted by permission.

Contents

Preface

St. Paul's greeting at the end of his letter to the Colossians (4:7ff) was the basis of my own introduction to this approach to reflection on the scriptures. It was part of a day of recollection and I remember wondering how on earth the group would manage to fill the hour and a half given for this spiritual excercise!

It was a most wonderful experience. Gently and reflectively, the story of those verses was opened to us and we to them and to each other. We sparked off one another, adding insights which we would not have dreamed of when first we looked at the passage. The story came to life; above all, the people of the story took new flesh, in the warmth and supportiveness of their relationships, in their awareness of the presence of the Lord and of his call to them to work together in his name. Gradually, fragments of our own stories were seen in new light and with new importance against that story.

Knowing *about* scripture is important in helping us approach scripture reflectively in this way. One of the strengths of this approach is that, although one can approach the scriptures with no formal background in biblical scholarship, it provides through the leader of the group simple but important insights in biblical scholarship which can have a deep effect on scriptural understanding.

Those who have shared the joy and enthusiasm of journeying in story with Dympna Magee will be glad that through this book that opportunity can be offered much more widely, as it well deserves to be.

Right Reverend John Rawsthorne,
Auxiliary Bishop of Liverpool

1

Introduction

Rediscovering the Scriptures

■ ■ ■ ■ ■ ■ ■ ■ ■ ■ ■ ■ ■ ■ ■

Why this book?

This book is about Jesus; it is about ourselves; it is about story. It offers a way for people to work together in groups and to reflect personally on scripture stories. It sees the Bible as the Story of the relationship between God and people, who are touched and changed by the encounter with God in their lives, and in the life of their communities.

This way of approaching the scriptures as story has much to offer, both to scholars and those with little or no formal background in biblical scholarship. The process acknowledges that people are all at different stages on their journey. Jesus took people where and as they were, and touched them in the ordinary circumstances of their lives. Through gospel stories, he touches people again, because when we hear these stories and are moved by them, Jesus is once more among us in his Word.

Reflecting upon the word of God is a basic Christian activity. As Christians, we need to recall, recollect, re-member the great happenings which called the Christian community into existence, and which continue to call us. In the stories of the Bible, we meet the God of crea-tion, the God of the Exodus, who brings his people into freedom, the God of the prophets and 'the God and Father of our Lord Jesus Christ' *(Ephesians 1:3)*. God is present in this word and we remember that Jesus told us that where two or three were gathered in his name, he would be among us. This is the power of the gospel.

One of the great gifts of the Holy Spirit to the Church in this century and particularly since the Second Vatican Council, is a rediscovery among Catholics of the riches which the Bible offers us. Reflection on the scriptures is food for the journey of all Christians. For many years, it was seen as the task and privilege only of theologians and scholars; or something belonging to other Christian traditions. We cannot affirm strongly enough that the scriptures belong to everyone.

The process of reflecting upon our lives, our personal and communal stories, in the light of the great Story of God and humankind is a rapidly developing area in modern spirituality. Many writers, such as John Shea in **Stories of God** and **Stories of Faith** and William Bausch in **Storytelling: Imagination and Faith**, work from the idea that this activity is both basic and essential to living the Christian life.

"Although it is necessary to start with the twists and turns of our own individual lives, we cannot stop there. On the journey of faith we do not travel alone. We walk with others who are our contemporaries. We also remember the journeys of those who came before us; and so we travel with tradition as a guide... The Church community has always accorded the Bible, and within the Bible the New Testament, and within the New Testament the Gospels, a special place. Therefore the relating of our personal lives to the tradition often takes the form of a dialogue with scripture." (John Shea, **Stories of Faith**, *St Thomas More Press,* Chicago, 1980, p.79)

Through this process of reflection, by ourselves and with others, we discover both our roots and our routes – where and from whom we have come and where and with whom we are journeying. The stories of Jesus provide the light for the roads we walk.

Why these stories?

This book is about Jesus. Obviously there are a great many stories about Jesus in the gospels, and it is always difficult to choose which ones to consider at any time. The first three stories in the book:

- *The Annunciation*
- *The Temptations*
- *The Transfiguration*

set the scene, so to speak. Jesus is the one whose coming is announced; he is the one who wrestles with the power of evil; he is the one to whom we must listen.

The next group or cluster of stories helps us to reflect on the words and works of Jesus so that we see him as prophet, liberator, feeder and storyteller. Finally, the Emmaus story is offered as the basis for two separate reflections in which we learn that the one who walks with us, and feeds us with Word and Bread is the prophet, liberator and feeder of the miracle stories, and the teller of tales in the parables.

Guidelines for a session reflecting specifically on aspects of our own personal stories, are also offered (p. 92). It is the responsibility of the group leader or the person using the book to decide when it is appropriate to have this session.

What do we mean by story?

Story can mean simply a narrative, an account or a recounting of an event, or an experience. There are many different kinds of narratives and stories. Some spring directly from people's lives and experience, and some are fictitious, for example, novels. For any story to be attractive or hold our interest, it must speak to something in us – an experience we have had, or are having, or perhaps desire to have – a fantasy, a dream. When we hear or read stories we become conscious that in some ways our experience is shared by other people, is common, and yet we are all unique, each having a personal story.

Personal story

Story can mean much more than a narrative. We speak of a person's own story. By this is meant :
- all the beliefs and values which a person holds
- his/her background
- what influences her/him
- the significant events and people in his/her life
- the traditions she/he values
- the dreams he/she aspires to.

All these are strands in that story. They come from the family, community and the outside world.

When I was a child, I heard very many stories from my parents about their childhood and their families; about what it was to be a member of this family with our particular values and treasures. Their values were passed on to me. My parents loved the Church and the Mass. They were vitally interested in politics, both Irish and international.

My parish and my teachers in school helped in this handing on of traditions. From them and from my own experience, I knew what it was to be a Catholic Christian, to be Irish, to be living in Belfast as part of a minority community. All this is now part of my story, part of what it is to be me.

I am also influenced by living in a world of rapid technological change. The influence of 'current stories' about politics, economics, world views, war and peace are also vitally significant in our lives. Yet each person has a story which is uniquely his or her own. There is a strand which is only mine, something which makes me, me, and no one else. I am a woman, but so are others. I am Irish, but so are others. I am a Catholic Christian, but so are others. But there is only one Dympna Magee. This is true of each of us and all of us.

Why do people tell stories?

People tell their stories to find meaning. We are all natural storytellers (though some are better than others). We need to put order on our experience, but at the same time we need to leave our experience open to future reflection and further telling. People tell the same stories over and over again in order to find meaning in them. We can see this very clearly when people in hospital retell the story of 'my operation'; when lovers tell over and over again how they met; when we are bereaved and tell stories of our lost ones to bring them back to us in some way. This is simply part of a process which is completely normal to human beings. We tell our stories because we have to.

The Christian story

Scripture story is part of the whole Christian story – the traditions, doctrines, stories, customs, prayer and liturgy which have been handed down through centuries of life in the Church. When we reflect on the scriptures, we are also bringing all these traditions with us – all these are part of the story we bring, an important strand in our lives.

God is active in our lives, through all these strands. As Christians, we believe that God touches us, each one, as an individual and as part of our communities. It is in the ordinary and extraordinary events of life (for example: work, relationships, love, death) that we meet God. Through reflection on this we come to know what God is doing in our lives and what he will do for us if we let him. We meet God in our experience (the strands) when we reflect upon it in faith.

The word my*th* is often used as a technical term to cover all this. This is not a term of disparagement, but rather a recognition of the importance of the story which lies behind someone's words and actions. It is essential to understand our own story, or own myth, but also to recognise the validity of another person's story, even that of our enemy. Although we believe that God is active in the strands of our own story, we also realise that our story is not perfect; there are flaws, things which need to be changed. Some things cannot be changed, but they can be viewed differently. Other parts of our story can be changed, for example: prejudices, wrong values.

Conversion

For Christians, the great story is the story of Jesus. When we reflect upon stories from his life, death and resurrrection and then reflect upon some aspect of our own story, we are called to change and grow, to become more like Jesus.

This process, central to Christian life, is called conversion. For some people, like Saint Paul, this appears as a once-and-for-all event, a radical change in the direction of life, but for most of us it is a fairly painful, lengthy and oft-repeated affair. At different times and stages on our faith journey the story of Jesus will show us the different areas of our life in need of conversion, a real change of heart.

At no time can we say that we have reached the end of this process. There **are always** some parts of our personal stories – resentments, prejudices, lack of forgiveness, poor self-image – that are in need of change. This work is not done in our heads, but in our hearts. To be converted, we must 'repent and believe in the gospel' *(Mark 1:15)* – the Good News which we hear in the scriptures.

Why this approach?

The twofold focus of the approach offered by this book is in

- seeing the scriptures as story
- affirming the value of the individual's own story.

We seek to know more about Jesus, so that we may know him better. We seek to hear what he is saying in our lives. We want to walk in his ways. We want our hearts to *burn within us* as he walks the roads of our lives with us. Knowledge of both head and heart have their place, but this approach is less concerned with the head and more with the heart and its reasons.

During the last ten years, I have worked with groups of people in Ireland and in England using this process. I have never been disappointed in their response. There is always a sense of excitement and of discovery. I always feel that Jesus does indeed again become present among his people as we share our thoughts and feelings about these stories. There is often laughter and sometimes tears, but one thing is certain –   hearts are always touched.

Who is this book for?

This book may be profitably used by someone on their own who wishes to reflect on these stories, or by groups of people in parishes or communities.

Working in groups

Commitment

A group may decide to meet weekly, fortnightly, monthly, according to its own needs. Although there are 13/14 sessions worked out in this book, the group may choose to do, for example, only the first three stories over a period of time, and then move on later to the next cluster of eight stories (perhaps during Lent); and then to the last two sessions and the final liturgy. There is progression in the stories, reflection questions and background material – so if you pick and choose there may be some difficulty in handling some of the questions and material.

It is always worthwhile to try to get a commitment to attend the meetings from as many people as possible. When the same people meet and share their thoughts and feelings an atmosphere of trust is built up. Of course no group should be completely closed to new members.

Using the questions and background material

Each story comes provided with a set of questions to help reflection, and some brief background notes. The group leader must read these thoroughly before the meeting, so as to be really familiar with them. The other members may read the material before or after the meeting according to their own preference. However, my own practice is to encourage people to meet the story without having read anything more than they already know, in order to make a personal, felt response to the story and the questions. This is to help us see and feel where in our lives (not just in our heads), the gospel touches us directly.

While each story has its own specific questions, there are four questions which basically underlie the whole process, and which a person using the book on his/her own, or a group, may choose to reflect upon rather than the specific questions for each story.

The four questions are:
1. What do I learn about Jesus from this story?
2. What is the image of God/who is God in this story?
3. Does this story have anything to say to me in my life?
4. What is this story calling me to change in my life? (see Conversion p. 10)

A group, or an individual, can reflect on any or all of these questions – or decide on questions of their own, if that is more helpful.

The meeting place

The place of meeting is important. The room should have the right temperature, be well lit and comfortable. Draughty parish halls or classrooms with infant-size chairs have brought to an early end many a good enterprise! Group members should sit in a circle so that everyone can be seen and heard.

To create a reflective atmosphere, the session could open with a piece of quiet music or a hymn, appropriate to the story for consideration; or simply a few moments of silent or quiet prayer.

Timing

Each session should last about one and a half hours.

↣ After a welcome and a prayer or hymn, the leader needs simply to name the story for the session. He/she, or someone else who has already been alerted, must read the story aloud, while the group **listens**.

Listening is important for we need to remind ourselves that these stories came originally from people with a strong oral tradition. If we listen carefully it can also help us to hear the story differently than before, to become aware of a word or phrase which perhaps had not struck us previously.

↣ The group members need the opportunity to then read the story silently for themselves.

↣ Next the group leader asks 'Does any word or phrase strike you?' 'What is the first thing you would like to say about the story?' This leads into a short time of sharing initial reflections and responses. People can be helped to speak if they share their responses in twos or threes before speaking in the larger group. This sharing of initial responses and questions is **essential** to the process – to help people to feel their way into the story, and into the session.

I suggest a timetable, as follows, but it is the responsibility of the group with the leader to be flexible about these times. If something is going well, go with it.

Suggested timetable of steps

1. Opening prayer/hymn — *5 minutes*
2. Reading story aloud and silently — *10 minutes*
3. Sharing initial responses — *10/15 minutes*
4. Small groups reflection on questions — *30 minutes*
5. Sharing reflections from small groups in larger group and input, using the background material, by the group leader — *25 minutes*
6. Closing prayer — *5 minutes*

Hints for group leaders

If the total group numbers up to seven or eight people there is no need to break up into small groups. This means that the session may be shorter or that a longer time than the suggested 30 minutes may be spent sharing thoughts and feelings on the questions (i.e. Steps 5 and 6 can be run together).

If the total group is more than eight or nine, then divide the members into groups of between five and eight, depending on numbers and the space available. Always encourage people to sit in a circle and lean inwards rather than outwards.

Each small group needs someone who is prepared to bring back the reflections of the group to the larger group. Always tell people exactly how long they have in the small group and encourage them to work all the questions.

In groups, all should be encouraged but not made to speak. The group leader needs to be aware of who is speaking and who is not. Do not allow a very talkative person to dominate the group. If there is a danger of this happening, simply say, 'Thank you' and move on to someone else. There is a school of thought which suggests going around the circle asking people to speak in turn, but this can be intimidating for a shy person. Group leaders can use their common sense! They can also remind themselves that they should not do all the talking, but if people are slow to begin to share, the leader can encourage by sharing his/her own response.

Reflection and discussion

What should be happening in these sessions is reflection and not discussion. Discussion has mainly to do with thinking, with decisions, facts and figures, with the head, for example, were there really 5,000 people present at the Feeding of the 5,000?

Reflection has much more to do with feelings, responses, with the meaning of a phrase, or the significance of a story in someone's life. When people are sharing something from their own life experience, or saying what a story says to them, there are no wrong answers. There is no question of contradiction, discussion or argument – simply an acceptance of the experiences being spoken about, and the reflection upon them. Each of us can speak only from our own personal experience, to which, it is hoped, the Gospel stories will speak. We cannot tell someone else what meaning this story should have for him or her. We can give fact, information and opinions, but in prayerful reflection, we can answer only for ourselves.

Between the sessions

At the end of the background material, there is a Personal Reflection or Meditation. This is not for sharing with the group, but is intended as a private exercise, to try to bring the power of the story into our personal lives. This is part of the process of conversion.

A final word

I hope you will enjoy reflecting on these stories, whether by yourself or in a group. I hope you will be encouraged to open your Bible and find other stories and other questions, so that the liberating power of God may fill all our lives and all our stories.

P A R T

2

Twelve Stories

■ ■ ■ ■ ■ ■ ■ ■ ■

In the sixth month the angel Gabriel was sent from God to a city of Galilee named Nazareth, to a virgin betrothed to a man whose name was Joseph, of the house of David; and the virgin's name was Mary. And he came to her and said, "Hail, O favoured one, the Lord is with you!" But she was greatly troubled at the saying, and considered in her mind what sort of greeting this might be. And the angel said to her, "Do not be afraid, Mary, for you have found favour with God. And behold, you will conceive in your womb and bear a son, and you shall call his name Jesus.

He will be great, and will be called the Son of the Most High; and the Lord God will give to him the throne of his father David, and he will reign over the house of Jacob forever; and of his kingdom there will be no end."

And Mary said to the angel, "How shall this be, since I have no husband?" And the angel said to her,

"The Holy Spirit will come upon you, and the power of the Most High will overshadow you; therefore the child to be born will be called holy, the Son of God.

And behold, your kinswoman Elizabeth in her old age has also conceived a son; and this is the sixth month with her who was called barren. For with God nothing will be impossible."

And Mary said, "Behold, I am the handmaid of the Lord; let it be to me according to your word." And the angel departed from her.

(*Luke 1:26-38*)

17

reflection • questions

1. What do you learn about:
- Mary
- Jesus
- God

from *this* story? (*not from other stories or traditions*).

2. Who is the central character? Why?

3. In groups of two or three, look in your Bible at the following stories:
- The Call of Moses (*Exodus 3:1-4:17*)
- The Call of Jeremiah (*Jeremiah 1:1-12*)
- *The Call of the Disciples* (*Luke 5:1-11*)

What similarities can you see in the Annunciation story and these stories?

4. What do we learn about discipleship from these stories?

background

1. Angels: messengers from God to humankind, they are frequently mentioned in the Old Testament,

e.g. *Genesis 19:1* **(two angels at Sodom)**
      1 Kings 19:5 **(angel speaks to Elijah)**

and less often in the New Testament,

e.g. *Mark 1:13* **(the Temptations of Jesus)**
      Luke 2:8-16 **(the shepherds)**.

They come usually to make an announcement on behalf of God, to bring help, or to punish. Some have names of their own:
- Gabriel: El (God) is strong.
- Michael: Who is like El (God)?
- Raphael: El (God) heals.

In scripture to speak of angels being present is a way of speaking of the power and presence of God.

2. Call narratives in the scriptures, both in the Old and the New Testaments, follow a particular pattern, including some or all of the following elements:

i   Setting
ii   Greeting
iii The Message/Call
iv   "Do not be afraid"
v   Objection/Reluctance
vi   Assurance
vii A Sign
viii Acceptance

3. Clusters of stories

When we look at a Bible story and other stories of which it reminds us (e.g. the Annunciation and the Call of Moses), we are able to see that stories are interlinked, because of their structure (*i.e. 'call' narratives*) or their theme (*healing, forgiveness, etc.*). We refer to these as clusters of stories.

A particular story rises out of a greater story, e.g. Creation stories, Exodus stories. There are background stories 'in behind' or 'over and above', particular stories. We need to try to see what story any particular story is coming out of.

4. God as a character in scripture

It is possible to see the Bible as a drama in two parts – the Old Testament as the first and the New Testament as the second. In the O.T. the plot is played out mainly between God and the people of Israel, with others (*e.g. Egyptians, Assyrians, etc*) having a supporting role. God is very definitely in centre stage. In the New Testament, God, as a biblical character, moves into the wings and Jesus is the character in centre stage, in relationship with his disciples, the crowds, the authorities and above all, with his father, his Abba, whose will he strives to carry out, whose perfect image he is. God is present in all Jesus stories, either directly referred to (*e.g. Luke 18:43*) or indirectly in metaphor (*e.g. 'the kingdom of heaven', Matthew 20:1; and the 'kingdom of God', Luke 19:11*), or quite clearly in the words and works of Jesus who speaks and acts in his time in the same manner as God was experienced by his people in the Old Testament (*e.g. Mark 6:30-44*).

5. Who is Jesus?

The identity of Jesus, Mary's Son, is presented very dramatically here. He is spoken of as the Messiah, in the line of David, and as the Son of God. His identity unfolds later in the gospel, e.g. in Peter's declaration in Luke 9: 20, "And he said to them, 'But who do you say that I am?' and Peter answered, 'The Christ of God'."

Mary is, in Luke's portrayal of her in the Gospel and the Acts, 'the favoured one' because she is the model disciple – she hears the word of God and does it. (*Cf. Luke 8: 21*)

personal reflection

(*between group sessions*)

Can you apply any of the elements of a 'call' narrative to your own faith journey?

> *a) Choose an incident, e.g. a disappointment, changing jobs, etc.*
>
> *b) How did you feel?*
>
> *c) Did you learn anything?*
>
> *d) Were you conscious of God's will at the time or did it become clearer on reflection?*

something to think about

...

Concerning the Divine Word

With the divinest word, the Virgin
Made pregnant, down the road
Comes walking, if you'll grant her
A room in your abode.

(St John of the Cross, trans. Roy Campbell,
Poems of St John of the Cross, *Collins Fount*,
1974, p. 89)

The Temptations of Jesus

■ ■ ■ ■ ■ ■ ■ ■ ■ ■ ■ ■ ■

And Jesus, full of the Holy Spirit, returned from the Jordan, and was led by the Spirit for forty days in the wilderness, tempted by the devil. And he ate nothing in those days; and when they were ended, he was hungry. The devil said to him, "If you are the Son of God, command this stone to become bread." And Jesus answered him, "It is written, 'Man shall not live by bread alone'." And the devil took him up, and showed him all the kingdoms of the world in a moment of time, and said to him, "To you I will give all this authority and their glory; for it has been delivered to me, and I give it to whom I will. If you, then, will worship me, it shall all be yours." And Jesus answered him, "It is written,

'You shall worship the Lord your God, and him
only shall you serve'."

And he took him to Jerusalem, and set him on the pinnacle of the temple, and said to him, "If you are the Son of God, throw yourself down from here; for it is written,

'He will give his angels charge of you, to guard
you.'
and
"On their hands they will bear you up, lest you
strike your foot against a stone'."

And Jesus answered him, "It is said, 'You shall not tempt the Lord your God'." and when the devil had ended every temptation, he departed from him until an opportune time.

(Luke 4:1-13)

reflection • questions

1. Does this story remind you of any other Bible story, either from the Old Testament or the New Testament? If so, why? In what ways?

2. From this story, how do you think Jesus saw his relationship with the Father in his mission?

3. How would you describe Jesus from this story? Agree as full a description as possible, for sharing in the large group.

4. Does this story raise any questions for the kind of Church we should be? Give practical examples from your own community.

remember:

1. Bible stories form clusters, i.e. they are related to one another, and each reminds us of other stories. For example, the temptation to turn the stones into bread reminds us of other 'bread' stories, like the feeding of the five thousand, or the feeding with manna in the desert. We can say, in fact, that the Bible has only one story, which is of the everloving and just relationship of God with a faithless and unjust people, who are called by God always to change – to conversion.

2. Metaphors and symbols

In coming to terms with the world of biblical story (and our own story), we need to be aware of the metaphors and symbols which are significant in these stories.

■ Symbols and metaphors are crucial in people's lives. They arise from experience. The most powerful symbols – light, darkness, struggle, journey, water – are universal because they arise from common experience, and provide a universal response to that experience. Symbols both rise from our experience, and speak to and enrich it. A symbol has the power to direct our thinking. Bible stories are rich in symbolism because they are concerned with the relationship of God and humankind.

■ We cannot see God or touch God and so we need to express our relationship symbolically. A symbol may be in the form or an object or a gesture. A symbol in word form may be called a **metaphor**. The metaphors used of God are personal and expressive of a relationship – shepherd, father, mother, king. A metaphor may be extended to become a whole story as in the case of the Emmaus story where it is not simply the events of an afternoon which are related but a whole lifetime's journey (see Emmaus story background p. 84).

■ We can only speak of God and our relationship with God in metaphors and symbols, because we cannot speak directly of God – our language is very limited.

Metaphors are part of that language. A metaphor is both true and not true, e.g. 'the Lord is my shepherd' is true, i.e. people experience God as loving and caring like a shepherd, but it is not **literally** true – i.e. cannot be scientifically proven – the Lord is not literally a shepherd.
Both Jews and Christians are biblical people, and share many of the metaphors in these stories, but hear and are aware of them in different ways.

3. Significant experiences

■ For Jews, the greatest experience of God was of the Exodus.
  • He brought them out of Egypt, 'out of the house of bondage' *(Deuteronomy 26:5b-10).*
  • 'He fed them in the desert, with manna' *(Deuteronomy 8:3-3; Exodus 16).*
  • 'They turned away from God, and worshipped the golden calf – a false god' *(Deuteronomy 9:7-21; Exodus 32:1-6).*
  • 'They grumbled against God; they 'put him to the test' – they failed to trust him *(Exodus 17:17).*

It was through this experience that they saw and experienced everything else in their history. We have inherited their story to some extent, because Jesus was a Jew.

■ For Christians, the most significant event is the life and death and especially the resurrection of Jesus. It is through that vision, and the hope which it gives us, that we hear the other stories of Jesus and see our own life stories and our death, and their meaning. When we hear bible stories, we must always be aware of these facts.

4. Jesus

In this story, we see Jesus as the hero in 'single combat' with the enemy,

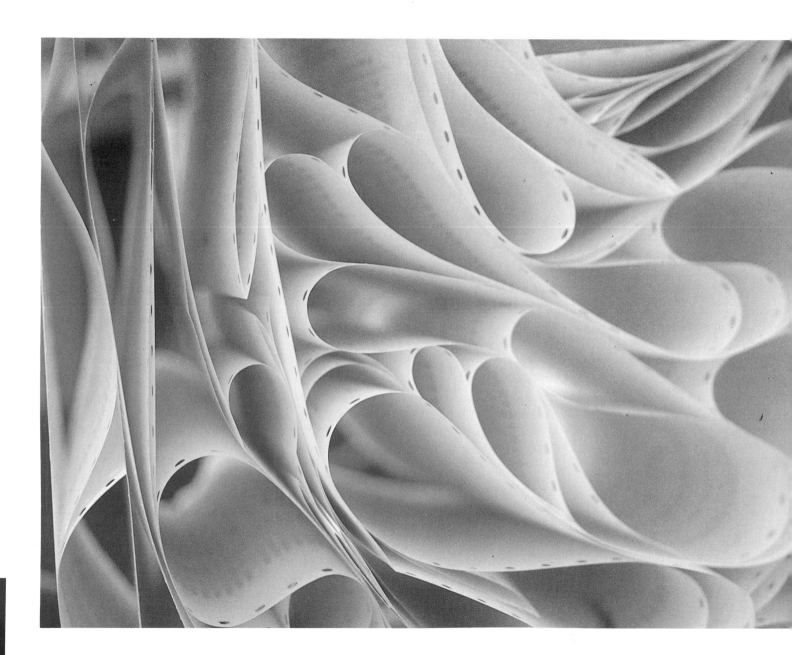

the tempter. The tempter is a familiar figure from the Old Testament, e.g. from the story of Job. God allows his Just One to be tempted in order to bring out a personal response, to show that his will is attuned to the will of God. The battle between the powers of evil and the powers of good goes on and on: this is clear from the phrase. 'until an opportune time'. Jesus commits himself completely to the battle. Luke's order of the temptations is therefore different to Matthew's, because Luke sees Jerusalem as central, and so he bring this story to its climax on the pinnacle of the Temple in Jerusalem.

■ The Jews looked back to the great king, David, and many expected a Messianic king, who would drive out the Romans, and restore Israel with great signs and wonders. All the temptations show clearly that Jesus rejects the idea of a wonder-working Messiah who will give people immediately what they want. Rather his way (and the way of his disciples) is one of humility and suffering, not political power. Jesus is indeed a king, but a **servant** king *(cf. John 6:15 and John 13:1-16)*.
From the temptations, it is clear that Jesus had no interest in
- possessions
- power
- prestige.

The greatest temptation is always to idolatry – basically, that is what all sin is. We put something or someone (usually ourselves) in the place God should occupy in our lives. Jesus refuses to do that. His response shows that he is singleminded in tuning his will to serve his Father's kingdom. He sees his mission as that of saving, of bringing the Father's Kingdom, not serving himself. His life will be one of service – it will take him to his agony and death. This will take place in Jerusalem, for Luke, the symbol of God's saving activity.

■ ■ ■ ■ ■ ■ ■ ■ ■ ■

something to think about

...

Psalm 95:1-9

O come, let us sing to the Lord;
    let us make a joyful noise to the rock
    of our salvation!
Let us come into his presence with thanksgiving
    let us make a joyful noise to him with songs of
    praise!
For the Lord is a great God,
    and a great King above all gods.
In his hand are the depths of the earth;
    the heights of the mountains are his also.
The sea is his, for he made it;
    for his hands formed the dry land.
O come, let us worship and bow down,
    let us kneel before the Lord, our Maker!
For he is our God,
    and we are the people of his pasture,
    and the sheep of his hand.
O that today you would hearken to his voice!
Harden not your hearts, as at Meribah,
    as on the day at Massah in the wilderness,
    when your father tested me,
    and put me to the proof,
    though they had seen my work.

The Transfiguration

■ ■ ■ ■ ■ ■ ■ ■ ■

Now about eight days after these sayings he took with him Peter and John and James, and went up on the mountain to pray. And as he was praying, the appearance of his countenance was altered, and his raiment became dazzling white. And behold two men talked with him, Moses and Elijah, who appeared in glory and spoke of his departure, which he was to accomplish at Jerusalem. Now Peter and those who were with him were heavy with sleep, and when they wakened they saw his glory and the two men who stood with him. And as the men were parting from him, Peter said to Jesus, "Master, it is well that we are here; let us make three booths, one for you and one for Moses and one for Elijah" – not knowing what he said.

As he said this, a cloud came and overshadowed them; and they were afraid as they entered the cloud. And a voice came out of the cloud, saying, "This is my Son, my Chosen; listen to him!" And when the voice had spoken, Jesus was found alone. And they kept silence and told no one in those days anything of what they had seen.

On the next day, when they had come down from the mountain, a great crowd met him.

(Luke 9:28-37)

reflection • questions

1. Who are the characters in the story?
What do you know about any of them?

2. What sets of relationships can you see in the story?
Make a list and comment.

3. What metaphors are present in the story?

4. What do we learn about prayer from the story?

5. Does this story ask us questions about our own prayer?

1. a) Moses and Elijah – the two greatest figures of the Old Testament.

Moses
- saw God face to face *(Deuteronomy 34:10)*
- led the people from slavery to freedom *(Exodus 14)*
- God gave the people his Law, through Moses *(Exodus 19 & 20)*
- God made the covenant with him *(Exodus 19:3-6)*
- God 'buried him' *(Deuteronomy 34:5-6)*

Elijah
- like Moses, met God on Horeb *(1 Kings 19)*
- challenged, in God's name, the evil of his day *(1 Kings 18, 19 & 21)*
- did not die but passed to heaven in a fiery chariot *(2 Kings 2:9-12)*

b) These two figures show how important it is to hold fast to what is good in tradition, e.g. worshipping one true God, keeping the commandments. The connection with Jesus is clear. The story speaks of Jesus' departure in Jerusalem – not his *death*, but his passing through death to life. It is **God** who brings this about, just as God buries Moses and brings Elijah to heaven.

2. 'This is my Son, my Chosen: listen to him!'
This marks not only the intimate relationship of Jesus and the Father *(cf. the Baptism of Jesus – Luke 3:21-22)*, but also shows that there is someone new to listen to, rather than Moses. Everything has changed. Listen! Hear! Shema! *(cf. Deuteronomy 6:4 foll.)*.

3. Metaphors

Some examples:

    i Mountain – the place to be near God
       (cf. Horeb and Sinai: Exodus 3, 1 Kings 19)

   ii Cloud – sign of God's presence
       (cf. Exodus 13)

  iii Tents – a sign of dwelling, of being with,
       being in the presence of
       (Exodus 40:34 ff.; Numbers 29:12 [Feast]; John 7:2)

4. Prayer

Jesus is changed, transfigured by the depth and power of his prayer. This is only one of many times when Jesus prayed, for example:

Luke 3:21;   Mark 1:35;   Luke 6:12;   Matthew 14:23;
Luke 11:1-4;   Luke 23:46;   Matthew 26:36-46.

Prayer was at the heart of his relationship with the Father. Through prayer, he became completely aware of the Father's will *(cf. Temptations)*. Prayer does not change God… it changes us. *(Weekday Preface Four: "You have no need of our praise, yet our desire to thank you is itself your gift. Our prayer of thanksgiving adds nothing to your greatness, but makes us grow in your grace, through Jesus Christ our Lord.")*

5. Reality

Peter wanted to stay up the mountain with Jesus, not to come down to reality, cf. after the resurrection *(Mark 16:6-7)* – as disciples, we must always be on the move, not staying in one place. Jesus brings them down the mountain again, to 'the crowd' – and an epileptic boy.

personal reflection

(between group sessions)

Either:

*In my prayer,
do I want to stay up the mountain,
away from reality,
or do I bring God into
the everyday events,
both good and bad, of my life?*

Or:

*Can you assess where on this
mountain the parish groups
with whom you are involved find
themselves?
What command is Jesus asking you
to listen to?*

29

something to think about

...

The Shema

Hear, O Israel: The Lord our God is one Lord;
and you shall love the Lord your God with all your Heart,
and with all your soul, and with all your might.
And these words which I command you this day
    shall be upon your heart;
and you shall teach them diligently to your children,
and shall talk of them when you sit in your house,
and when you walk by the way, and when you lie down,
    and when you rise.
And you shall bind them as a sign upon your hand,
and they shall be as frontlets between your eyes.
And you shall write them on the doorposts of your house
    and on your gates.

(Deuteronomy 6:4-9)

Jesus and the Woman in the Synagogue

■ ■ ■ ■ ■ ■ ■ ■ ■ ■ ■

Now he was teaching in one of the synagogues on the sabbath. And there was a woman who had had a spirit of infirmity for eighteen years; she was bent over and could not fully straighten herself. And when Jesus saw her, he called her and said to her, "Woman, you are freed from your infirmity." And he laid his hands upon her, and immediately she was made straight, and she praised God. But the ruler of the synagogue, indignant because Jesus had healed on the sabbath, said to the people, "There are six days on which work ought to be done; come on those days and be healed, and not on the sabbath day." Then the Lord answered him, "You hypocrites! Does not each of you on the sabbath untie his ox or his ass from the manger, and lead it away to water it? And ought not this woman, a daughter of Abraham whom Satan bound for eighteen years, be loosed from this bond on the sabbath day?" As he said this, all his adversaries were put to shame; and all the people rejoiced at all the glorious things that were done by him.

(Luke 13:10-17)

reflection • questions

1. Who are the characters in this story?

2. What is Jesus offering to:
- the woman
- the synagogue official?

3. What do you find attractive about Jesus in this story? What do you find challenging about him?

4. What are the dangers for Jesus in changing this situation?

5. Is there any danger for you in changing a situation

    e.g.   at work?

         in the family?

1. Sabbath and Law

In the Old Testament, the principle was laid down that one day in seven should be kept as a day holy to God. In Genesis 2:2-3, we are told that God finished his work of creation and rested on the seventh day, and for that reason, the seventh day was to be hallowed.

When the Ten Commandments were given to the people on Mount Sinai, the sabbath was again called holy, because it was the day God rested. But an additional reason is given here for keeping the sabbath *(Deuteronomy 5:15)*, that man and woman may rest. As with the other commandments, this springs from the Exodus experience – as God released his people from slavery, in Egypt, so Israel must show mercy to those who work for them. The sabbath clearly was 'made for man': an opportunity to reflect on being an Exodus person.

The celebration of the sabbath is the sign of being a free people – of re-membering God's redeeming action, and therefore a cause of joy for the people of Israel.

The keeping of the sabbath was always a matter of great importance. Jeremiah warned that Jerusalem would be destroyed if the sabbath was not kept, but would flourish and prosper if it was. However, some of the other prophets railed against the outward observance of sabbath law, while God was not truly worshipped in the hearts and social behaviour of his people *(cf. Amos 5:21-24)*. However, the custom grew up among those interpreting the Law *(the Pharisees in the time of Jesus)* to draw up minute and burden-some laws about the keeping of the sabbath.

It was against this that Jesus spoke and acted. He revered the sabbath as a holy day, but he castigated those who put burdens on people through adding unnecessarily to the Law. Jesus knew that laws are essentially for freedom, not for slavery. His anger was directed against those who used the Law to enslave rather than to direct and free.

2. The Synagogue

The synagogue in the scriptures was both the gathering of people in a locality for prayer and worship, and the gathering place. During the Exile *(6th century B.C.)*, when the Temple in Jerusalem could not be used for worship, the synagogue grew in importance as a place of instruction in the scriptures and for prayer.

The gospels often speak of Jesus in the synagogue on the sabbath day *(e.g. Luke 4:16; Mark 1:21)*. As a devout Jew, it would have been unthinkable for him not to go there on the sabbath. We know from Luke 4:16 that he was invited to speak in the synagogue in Nazareth, and caused a riot there, and we know that he cured not only the bent woman of this story in a synagogue but also a man with a withered hand *(Luke 6:6-11)*.

3. Jesus and the sick

Often in the gospels, we see the concern of Jesus for the sick – perhaps this woman is a symbol for them, and for all those to whom Jesus ministered. In the time of Jesus, sickness was regarded as a punishment for sin *(cf. John 9, the Blind Man)*. A sick person was regarded as a living sign of God's displeasure, and therefore caused a stigma of guilt which made her or him an outcast from the community. In healing the woman, Jesus is not only restoring her to health but giving her standing again in the community.

personal reflection

(between group sessions)

What is this story calling you to let go of?

35

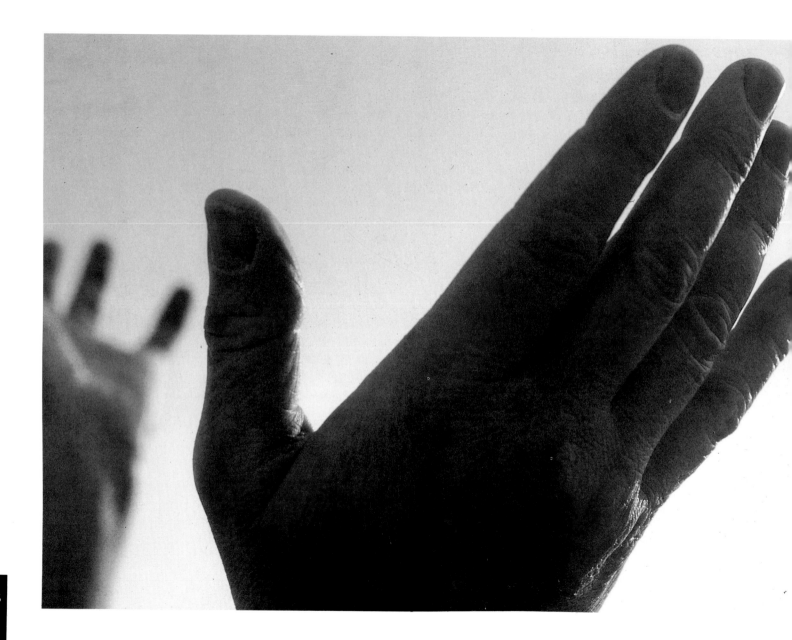

something to think about

...

The Woman's Story

A bundle of dirty rags,
I must have looked,
To those who passed and didn't really see me.
Bent over, a thing despised.
Yet hope kept me coming every Sabbath,
to crouch in a corner,
Though the holy people said
that God would never hear a sinner's prayer.
But suddenly a voice called:
"Woman, Woman?"
Could he be speaking to me?
Gently hands upon me.
I stood upright.
And saw him, face to face.

Jesus and the Samaritan Woman

■ ■ ■ ■ ■ ■ ■ ■ ■ ■ ■ ■ ■

Now when the Lord knew that the Pharisees had heard that Jesus was making and baptizing more disciples than John (although Jesus himself did not baptize, but only his disciples), he left Judea and departed again to Galilee. He had to pass through Samaria. So he came to a city of Samaria, called Sychar, near the field that Jacob gave to his son Joseph. Jacob's well was there, and so Jesus, wearied as he was with his journey, sat down beside the well. It was about the sixth hour.

There came a woman of Samaria to draw water. Jesus said to her, "Give me a drink". For his disciples had gone away into the city to buy food.

The Samaritan woman said to him, "How is it that you, a Jew, ask a drink of me, a woman of Samaria?" For Jews have no dealings with Samaritans.

Jesus answered her, "If you knew the gift of God, and who it is that is saying to you, 'Give me a drink', you would have asked him, and he would have given you living water."

The woman said to him, "Sir, you have nothing to draw with, and the well is deep; where do you get that living water? Are you greater than our father Jacob, who gave us the well, and drank from it himself, and his sons, and his cattle?"

Jesus said to her, "Everyone who drinks of this water will thirst again, but whoever drinks of the water that I shall give him will never thirst; the water that I shall give him will become in him a spring of water welling up to eternal life."

The woman said to him, "Sir, give me this water, that I may not thirst, nor come here to draw."

Jesus said to her, "Go, call your husband, and come here."

The woman answered him, "I have no husband."

Jesus said to her, "You are right in saying 'I have no husband'; for you have had five husbands, and he whom you now have is not your husband; this you said truly."

The woman said to him, "Sir, I perceive that you are a prophet. Our fathers worshipped on this mountain; and you say that in Jerusalem is the place where men ought to worship."

Jesus said to her, "Woman, believe me, the hour is coming when neither on this mountain nor in Jerusalem will you worship the Father. You worship what you do not know; we worship what we know, for salvation is from the Jews. But the hour is coming, and now is, when the true worshippers will worship the Father in spirit and truth, for such the Father seeks to worship him. God is spirit, and those who worship him must worship in spirit and truth."

The woman said to him, "I know that Messiah is coming (he who is called Christ); when he comes, he will show us all things."

Jesus said to her, "I who speak to you am he."

Just then his disciples came. They marvelled that he was talking with a woman, but none said, "What do you wish?" or "Why are you talking with her?" So the woman left her water jar, and went away into the city, and said to the people, "Come, see a man who told me all that I ever did. Can this be the Christ?" They went out of the city and were coming to him.

Meanwhile the disciples besought him, saying, "Rabbi, eat." But he said to them, "I have food to eat of which you do not know." So the disciples said to one another, "Has anyone brought him food?" Jesus said to them, "My food is to do the will of him who sent me, and to accomplish his work. Do you not say, 'There are yet four months, then comes the harvest?' I tell you, lift up your eyes, and see how the fields are already white for harvest. He who reaps receives wages, and gathers fruit for eternal life, so that sower and reaper may rejoice together. For here the saying holds true, 'One sows and another reaps.' I sent you to reap that for which you did not labour; others have laboured, and you have entered into their labour."

Many Samaritans from that city believed in him because of the woman's testimony, 'He told me all that I ever did.' So when the Samaritans came to him, they asked him to stay with them; and he stayed there two days. And many more believed because of his word. They said to the woman, "It is no longer because of your words that we believe, for we have heard for ourselves, and we know that this is indeed the Saviour of the world."

After the two days he departed to Galilee.

(*John 4:1-43*)

reflection • questions

1. Look carefully at the conversation between Jesus and the woman.
What do you learn from this about:
  • Jesus?
  • the woman?

2. Can you see stages in the woman's understanding of who Jesus is?
How does she show this?

3. What does Jesus do for the woman?
What does he make possible for her?

4. What do you see as the significant metaphors or symbols in this story?

5. Can you hear any of the stories that a Jew would hear in the background of this story (e.g. Jacob's well)?
What stories are we, as Christians, reminded of?

background

1. Samaritans

Samaritan is the name given in the New Testament to the inhabitants of Samaria, but the name Samaritan meant far more than that, and had very deep religious significance. The Jews regarded the Samaritans as heretics and despised them even more than pagans. The Samaritans themselves were descendants of a mixed population of Israelites, who survived the deportations to Assyria in the 8th Century B.C., and foreign people settled in Israel by the Assyrians. When the Temple in Jerusalem was rebuilt by the exiles who had returned from Babylon, not only would the Samaritans have nothing to do with them, they actively opposed its reconstruction. Eventually (the exact date is not known), the Samaritans built their own temple on Mount Gerezim ('this mountain' referred to be the Samaritan woman in the story). This split them completely from the Jews.

■ Samaritan beliefs

The Samaritans accepted only the Pentateuch (the Five Books of Moses) as canonical. They had (and have) a high priest. They had a belief in a messiah (cf. the woman's words to Jesus), but it was rather vague.

■ The hostility between Jews and Samaritans is very clear in the bible, as can be seen in this story, where even an ordinary village woman knows how unlikely it is for a Jewish man to ask a Samaritan woman for a drink. She shows herself well-versed in the Samaritan-Jewish theological difficulties about where worship should take place.

Perhaps this may help us begin to appreciate how shocking it was for Jesus to tell the parable of the Good Samaritan.

2. The sixth hour

This is noon and a very unusual time for a woman to go to draw water. The fact that she was there at that time is usually taken as an indication of her being an outcast, even in her own community, since women went as a group to draw water early in the morning.

The fact of her being sent by Jesus to her townspeople with the 'good news' restores her to a status of respect in the community, and indeed makes her an apostle.

3. The importance of 'well' stories

> e.g. Hagar meets the angel of God *(Genesis 21:8-21)*
> Jacob meets Rachel *(Genesis 29:1-20)*
> Moses and the daughters of the priest of Midian *(Exodus 2:15-22)*

■ *Living Water* (cf. Stories of 'wells' and the 'water from the rock' in *Exodus 17*)

It is very difficult for us to appreciate the significance of water for the people of the Near East both then and now. Occasionally, we can share a little of their experience, perhaps during a water shortage when standpipes are brought into use, or when there is a scare over the purity of our drinking water. We expect a clean and plentiful water supply as a matter of right. For people in the Near East, it is a matter for tremendous gratitude, because it means hard work, and living with a great deal of uncertainly as to whether there will be sufficient water or not.

The ruler of a desert country in the 1950s, having been told by surveyors that under his sandy kingdom were millions of tonnes of oil, said, "Would it were water!"

(between group sessions)

1. Has my understanding of Jesus changed?
   Grown?
   In what way?

2. Does this story challenge my image of Jesus?
   Or reassure me?

something to think about

...

A Drink of Water

She came every morning to draw water
Like an old bat staggering up the field:
The pump's whooping cough, the bucket's clatter
The slow diminuendo as it filled,
Announced her. I recall
Her grey apron, the pocked white enamel
Of the brimming bucket, and the treble
Creak of her voice like the pump's handle.
Nights when a full moon lifted past her gable
It fell back through her window and would lie
Into the water set out on the table.
Where I have dipped to drink again, to be
Faithful to the admonishment on her cup,
Remember the Giver fading off the lip.

(Seamus Heaney, **Field Work**, *Faber*, 1979)

Jesus and the Gerasene Demoniac

▪ ▪ ▪ ▪ ▪ ▪ ▪ ▪ ▪

They came to the other side of the sea, to the country of the Gerasenes. And when he had come out of the boat, there met him out of the tombs a man with an unclean spirit, who lived among the tombs; and no one could bind him any more, even with a chain; for he had often been bound with fetters and chains, but the chains he wrenched apart, and the fetters he broke in pieces; and no one had the strength to subdue him. Night and day among the tombs and on the mountains he was always crying out, and brusing himself with stones. And when he saw Jesus from afar he ran and worshipped him and crying out with a loud voice he said, "What have you to do with me, Jesus, Son of the Most High God? I adjure you by God, do not torment me." For he had said to him, "Come out of the man, you unclean spirit!"

And Jesus asked him, "What is your name?" He replied, "My name is Legion; for we are many." And he begged him eagerly not to send them out of the country.

Now a great herd of swine was feeding there on the hillside; and they begged him, "Send us to the swine, let us enter them." So he gave them leave. And the unclean spirits came out, and entered the swine; and the herd, numbering about two thousand, rushed down the steep bank into the sea, and were drowned in the sea.

The herdsmen fled, and told it in the city and in the country. And people came to see what it was that had happened. And they came to Jesus, and saw the demoniac sitting there, clothed and in his right mind, the man who had had the legion; and they were afraid. And those who had seen it told what had happened to the demoniac and to the swine. And they began to beg Jesus to depart from their neighbourhood. And, as he was getting into the boat, the man who had been possessed with demons begged him that he might be with him. But he refused and said to him, "Go home to your friends, and tell them how much the Lord has done for you, and how he has had mercy on you." And he went away and began to proclaim in the Decapolis how much Jesus had done for him; and all men marvelled.

(Mark 5:1-20)

1. What images of slavery and death are there in this story?

2. What images of freedom and life are there in this story?

3. a) How does Jesus deal with the man:
- possessed?
- cured?

b) What does Jesus ask him to do?

4. What does our society do:
- with people with whom it cannot cope?
- with people who change?

5. What is 'the other side' for me? e.g. in 'them and us' situations.

background

1. Who is he?

This story follows on directly from the account of the calming of the storm, which ends "Who then is this that even the wind and the sea obey him?" It is followed by the cure of the woman with the haemorrhage and the raising of Jairus' daughter and the visit by Jesus to 'his own country' where people asked, "Where did this man get all this?" *(Matthew 6:1ff.)*. The central concern of this part of Mark's gospel is in fact to put the question of the identity of Jesus to his hearers – to uncover his story.

2. Gerasene

Gerasenes were inhabitant of Geresa – a city to the north east of the Sea of Galilee – a city which may be confused with Gadara, of the 'Ten Towns' (the Decapolis) in eastern Palestine. The inhabitants were pagans, not the kind of people with whom Jews normally dealt, if they could avoid doing so. The fact that the story tells us that they were keepers of pigs – and in huge numbers – gives us some clues about how repugnant their lifestyle would seem to Jews.

3. Pigs/swine

These were regarded as unclean by the Jews *(Leviticus 11:17; Deuteronomy 14:8)*. In the period of the Maccabees, not to eat pork became a great symbol of true Jewish religious observance. In this story of the cure of the demoniac, it is the symbolism of swine as an appropriate dwelling place for an 'unclean spirit' which is significant. Neither the unclean demon nor the unclean swine can be in the presence of the Messiah.

4. Hearing the enemy's story

Each of us has a story which is valuable. To refuse to hear the story of another is to regard her or him as an enemy; conversely, to regard someone as an enemy is to refuse to listen to her or his story. To hear and respect my enemy's story means that I can no longer regard her or him as my enemy. Jesus was open to the story of even those most despised by his own people.

personal reflection

(between group sessions)

This week,
try to listen to the story
of someone you would not normally
listen to.

something to think about

...

Eyewitness

"Dark cliffs, evening clouds rolling in and us blown off course – a strange and eerie place for Jews, especially among these pagans – they even keep pigs. But most strange of all, a madman, utterly possessed and roaring and shouting. The Master just told the demons to come out, in that commanding tone of voice he has, and they did and straight into a herd of pigs and into the sea. I must admit I was terrified, but there was the madman all calm, clothed and sitting at the feet of Jesus looking at him with big hopeful eyes, while everyone else was in a state. What a turn around!

The people started shouting at Jesus and us to go away – I suppose the Master's power must have frightened them. It scares me sometimes. The man wanted to come with us, but the Lord told him to go and tell others what had been done for him. I'm glad in a way that he didn't come with us, because I wonder how he would have fitted in. Could we have coped with someone so strange?

I don't know. Sometimes it's hard enough coping with the Master himself!"

Jesus and the Man Born Blind

■ ■ ■ ■ ■ ■ ■ ■ ■

As he passed by, he saw a man blind from his birth. and his disciples asked him, "Rabbi, who sinned, this man or his parents, that he was born blind?" Jesus answered, "It was not that this man sinned, or his parents, but that the works of God might be made manifest in him. We must work the works of him who sent me while it is day; night comes, when no one can work. As long as I am in the world, I am the light of the world." As he said this, he spat on the ground and made clay of the spittle and anointed the man's eyes with the clay, saying to him, "Go, wash in the pool of Siloam" (which means Sent). So he went and washed and came back seeing. The neighbours and those who had seen him before as a beggar, said, "Is not this the man who used to sit and beg?" Some said, "It is he." Others said, "No, but he is like him." He said, "I am the man." They said to him, "Then how were your eyes opened?" He answered, "The man called Jesus made clay and anointed my eyes and said to me, 'Go to Siloam and wash'; so I went and washed and received my sight." They said to him, "Where is he?" He said, "I do not know."

They brought to the Pharisees the man who had formerly been blind. Now it was a Sabbath day when Jesus made the clay and opened his eyes. The Pharisees again asked him how he had received his sight. And he said to them,

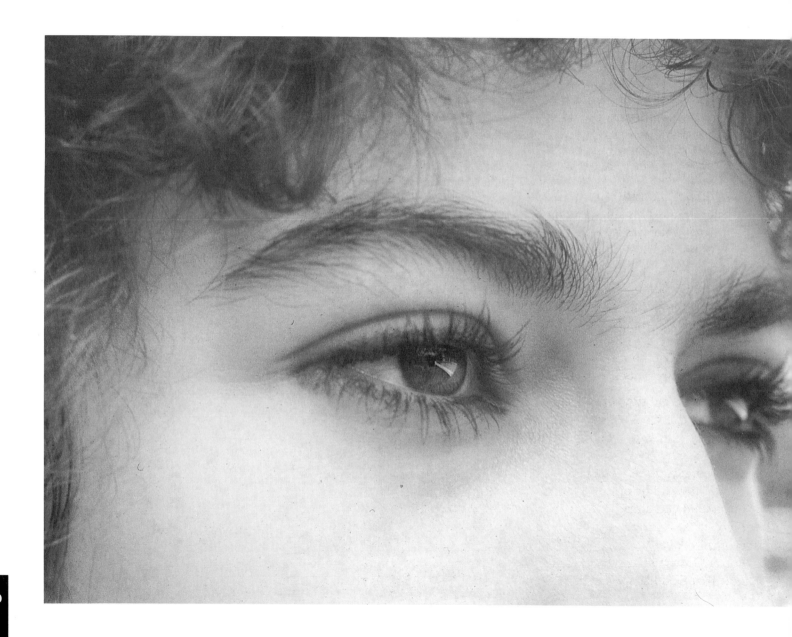

"He put clay on my eyes, and I washed, and I see." Some of the Pharisees said, "This man is not from God, for he does not keep the Sabbath." But others said, "How can a man who is a sinner do such signs?" There was a division among them. So they again said to the blind man, "What do you say about him, since he has opened your eyes?" He said, "He is a prophet."

The Jews did not believe that he had been blind and had received his sight until they called the parents of the man who had received his sight, and asked them, "Is this your son, who you say was born blind? How then does he now see?" His parents answered, "We know that this is our son, and that he was born blind; but how he now sees, we do not know nor do we know who opened his eyes. Ask him; he is of age, he will speak for himself." His parents said this because they feared the Jews, for the Jews had already agreed that if anyone should confess him to be Christ, he was to be put out of the synagogue. Therefore, his parents said, "He is of age, ask him."

So for the second time they called the man who had been blind, and said to him, "Give God the praise; we know that this man is a sinner." He answered, "Whether he is a sinner, I do not know; one thing I know, that though I was blind, now I see." They said to him, "What did he do to you? How did he open your eyes?" He answered them, "I have told you already, and you would not listen. Why do you want to hear it again? Do you, too, want to become his disciples?" And they reviled him, saying, "You are his disciple, but we are disciples of Moses. We know that God has spoken to Moses, but as for this man, we do not know where he comes from." The man answered, "Why this is a marvel! You do not know where he comes from, and yet he opened my eyes. We know that God does not listen to sinners, but if anyone is a worshipper of God and does his will, God listens to him. Never since the world began has it been heard that anyone opened the eyes of a man born blind. If this man were not from God, he could do nothing." They answered him, "You were born in utter sin, and would you teach us?" And they cast him out.

Jesus heard that they had cast him out, and having found him, he said, "Do you believe in the Son of Man?" He answered, "And who is he, sir, that I may believe in him?" Jesus said to him, "You have seen him, and it is he who speaks to you." He said, "Lord, I believe," and he worshipped him. Jesus said, "For judgement I came into this world, that those who do not see may see, and that those who see may become blind." Some of the Pharisees near him heard this, and they said to him, "Are we also blind?" Jesus said to them, "If you were blind, you would have no guilt; but now that you say, 'We see', your guilt remains."

(*John 9:1-41*)

reflection • questions

1. a) How many times does the word *blind* appear in this story? What other words in the story are associated with it?

b) What words in the story would you say are in contrast to *blind*?

c) What do the answers to these questions tell you about the purpose of this story?

2. Can you see any development in the blind man's understanding of Jesus?

3. This is a story where Jesus is seen in conflict with the authorities: what other stories are you reminded of?

4. What would inevitably happen to Jesus?

5. Imagine you are a Pharisee and are discussing the events of this story afterwards. What feelings do you have about Jesus? *(This might be done in pairs in the group situation.)*

background

1. Metaphors and symbols

(see p. 22)
It is important to remember how significant these are in story. There are many in this story, particularly light and darkness, sight and blindness.

2. Light

It is a constant theme in St John's gospel, e.g. John 1:4-5 and John 1:9. Jesus speaks of himself as 'the light of the world', John 8:12 and John 9:5.

3. The Council of Jamnia

(cf John 9:22)
'His parents said this because they feared the Jews, for the Jews had already said that if anyone should confess him to be Christ, he was to be put out of the synagogue.' The final definitive break between the Jews and Jewish Christians in Palestine came at the Council of Jamnia at the end of the first century, when in fact the Christians were 'put out of the synagogue'. They were regarded by the Jews as an heretical sect.

We need to remind ourselves that all the gospel stories were told, and then written **after** the death and resurrection of Jesus, and in the light of these events. The gospel accounts are not the first telling of these stories. They are reflections of the experience of the communities in which and for whom they were told. There seems no doubt among scholars that John's is the latest of the four gospels to be written. The community from which it came was no doubt suffering from begin 'put out of the synagogue'. This story is written in the light of that experience.

4. Levels of story

There is only **one story in the Bible**, told in many different ways and modes (cf. Temptations, p. 22). John Shea says, "It is a story of a God, boundless in justice, who will not go away, and a people, holding in hope, who will not give up". We might say it is a story of a God who constantly frees his people, so that they, in turn, become passionately devoted to freeing others, which is the work of justice.

Among the many different ways of telling this story are creation stories, exodus stories, prophecy, miracle stories, parables, passion and resurrection stories. In this story, which at one level is clearly a miracle story, we can also see a creation story. In the first account of creation in Genesis 1, the first thing God does is to create light. At the pinnacle of his creation God places humankind – 'So God created man in his own image, in the image of God he created him: male and female he created them' *(Genesis 1:27)*.

The second account of creation in Genesis 2 tells us that God forms man from his own breath and the dust of the earth *(Genesis 2:7)*. In this story of the cure of the man born blind, Jesus makes clay from the earth and from his own spittle and anoints the man's eyes – the man then walks in the light, and enjoys newness of life.

Those familiar with the Genesis accounts of creation would be reminded of them here by the words and actions of Jesus.

It can be helpful in understanding scripture stores, if we can link the stories with each other, and see different kinds of stories within them, e.g. when the woman in the synagogue is freed from her infirmity, there are over-tones of Exodus.

There are always other stories inside stories. (cf. The Annunciation, p. 18) Even when we reflect upon a story to try to draw out its meaning for us today, we have not, and cannot exhaust its meaning. The story and our lives are enriched by our reflection, but we need to remember that stories are open-ended.

Imagine yourself as one of the characters in the story:

- *the blind man*

- *one of his parents*

- *a Pharisee*

- *Jesus*

- *a disciple.*

Tell yourself the story from the point of view of the character you have chosen.
What do you learn about:

- *yourself?*

- *your own blindness?*

- *Jesus?*

5. Stages of Faith

Many theologians and educationalists agree that our faith goes through various stages through life's journey. We develop our understanding of who God is and our relationship with him, and what Jesus and the Church mean to us. Putting this theory of stages very simply, we can see three main stages.

- First: we take on the faith story, the tradition which we inherit from our parents and community.
- Second: we often question the inherited story, trying to find our own answers to our own questions, rather than accepting someone else's answers. This stage, frequently, but not always, happens during adolescence. It is part of the process of growing in faith.
- Third: this stage, if and when we reach it, is when we are said to 'own' our faith. We have reached a point where we decide that we will embrace the Christian life, perhaps despite difficulties and problems, and conscious of our shortcomings. Even at this stage of faith, we will not have all the answers, but we acknowledge the need to reflect upon and even change our ideas and images of God, Jesus, the Church and so on.

something to think about

...

The blindness of the Pharisees was not innocent. They were not like people who genuinely want to see and try hard to understand but because of their education and social conditioning are simply unable to see. This kind of blindness can be cured with time as in the case of Nicodemus. But there is another kind of blindness. It is the blindness of those who do not want to see or, more precisely, the blindness of those who are blind to their own blindness and who are therefore convinced that they can see perfectly clearly. Most of the Pharisees, it seems, were like that. When Jesus points out that they are blind, they are astonished. 'We are not blind, surely?' Jesus replied: 'Blind? If you were, you would not be guilty; but since you say, 'We see', your guilt remains.' *(John 9:4—41)* Today we call it culpable blindness ... the element of self-deception or blindness ... is present in all sin.

(Albert Nolan, **God in South Africa**, *CIIR*, 1988, p. 40)

The Raising of Lazarus

Now a certain man was ill, Lazarus of Bethany, the village of Mary and her sister Martha. It was Mary who anointed the Lord with ointment and wiped his feet with her hair, whose brother Lazarus was ill. So the sisters sent to him, saying, "Lord, he whom you love is ill."
But when Jesus heard it, he said, "This illness is not unto death; it is for the glory of God, so that the Son of God may be glorified by means of it."

Now Jesus loved Martha and her sister and Lazarus. So when he heard that he was ill, he stayed two days longer in the place where he was. Then after this he said to the disciples, "Let us go into Judea again."
The disciples said to him, "Rabbi, the Jews were but now seeking to stone you, and are you going there again?"
Jesus answered, "Are there not twelve hours in the day? If anyone walks in the day, he does not stumble because he sees the light of this world. But if anyone walks in the night, he stumbles because the light is not in him."
Thus he spoke, and then he said to them, "Our friend Lazarus has fallen asleep, but I go to awake him out of sleep." The disciples said to him, "Lord, if he has fallen asleep, he will recover." Now Jesus had spoken of his death, but they thought that he meant taking rest in sleep. Then Jesus told them plainly, "Lazarus is dead; and for your sake I am glad that I was not there, so that you many believe. But let us go to him." Thomas, called the Twin, said to his fellow disciples, "Let us also go, that we may die with him."

Now when Jesus came, he found that Lazarus had already been in the tomb four days. Bethany was near Jerusalem, about two miles off, and many of the Jews had come to Martha and Mary to console them concerning their brother. When Martha heard that Jesus was coming, she went and met him, while Mary sat in the house. Martha said to Jesus, "Lord, if you had been here, my brother would not have died. And even now I know that whatever you ask from God, God will give you." Jesus said to her, "Your brother will rise again." Martha said to him, "I know that he will rise again in the resurrection at the last day." Jesus said to her, "I am the resurrection and the life; he who believes in me, though he die, yet shall he live, and whoever lives and believes in me shall never die. Do you believe this?" She said to him, "Yes, Lord, I believe that you are the Christ, the Son of God, he who is coming into the world."

When she had said this, she went and called her sister, Mary, saying quietly, "The Teacher is here and is calling for you."

And when she heard it, she rose quickly and went to him. Now Jesus had not yet come to the village, but was still in the place where Martha had met him. When the Jews who were with her in the house, consoling her, saw Mary rise quickly and go out, they followed her, supposing that she was going to the tomb to weep there. Then Mary, when she came where Jesus was and saw him, fell at his feet, saying to him, "Lord, if you had been here, my brother would not have died." When Jesus saw her weeping, and the Jews who came with her also weeping, he was deeply moved in spirit and troubled, and he said, "Where have you laid him?" They said to him, "Lord, come and see." Jesus wept. So the Jews said, "See how he loved him!" But some of them said, "Could not he who opened the eyes of the blind man have kept this man from dying?"

Then Jesus, deeply moved again, came to the tomb; it was a cave, and a stone lay upon it. Jesus said, "Take away the stone." Martha, the sister of the dead man, said to him, "Lord, by this time there will be an odour, for he has been dead four days." Jesus said to her, "Did I not tell you that if you would believe, you would see the glory of God?" So they took away the stone. And Jesus lifted up his eyes and said, "Father, I thank thee that thou hast heard me. I knew that thou hearest me always, but I have said this on account of the people standing by, that they may believe that thou didst send me." When he had said this, he cried with a loud voice, "Lazarus, come out." The dead man came out, his hands and feet bound with bandages, and his face wrapped with a cloth. Jesus said to them, "Unbind him, and let him go."

(*John 11:1-44*)

reflection • questions

1. What relationships can you see in this story?
Why are they important?

2. What titles are used for Jesus?
What do you think they mean?

3. If we had only this story of Jesus (and **no** other),
what would we learn:
   • about him?
   • about faith?

4. As Jesus unbinds Lazarus, to what does he bind himself?
(Clue: Look at the words of Thomas.)

1. Binding/unbinding

The God of the Bible is a God of life, a God who frees, unbinding people from whatever situation keeps them in slavery – sin, oppression, hunger, death. Some of the outstanding examples of this in the Old Testament are, of course, the Exodus, the unbinding of Isaac *(Genesis 21)*, Elijah and the widow's son *(1 Kings 17)*, the bringing back of the people from Exile. But, as God unbinds people, so he binds himself to them.

2. The Covenant

The Covenant with the people of Israel made at Mount Sinai *(Exodus 19: 3-6)* and renewed so often through the prophets had one central theme: "I will be their God and they will be my people" *(John 31:33)*. It was always clear that God **freely** bound himself to this covenant – out of love *(Deuteronomy 7:6-10)*. It is an act of graciousness and generosity on God's part, not an agreement between two equals.

The Covenant at Sinai was not the first mentioned in the Old Testament. God made a covenant with all humankind through Noah *(Genesis 9)* and with Abraham *(Genesis 15 and 17)*. It is the covenant with Abraham which forms the original basis of the Hebrew relationship with God.

This covenant relationship, this binding in love, is alluded to by Jesus when he calls his blood 'the blood of the covenant ' *(Mark 14:24)* and speaks of 'the new covenant in my blood' *(Luke 22:20)*.

The Incarnation is above all the sign of God's binding of himself to us in love, to unbind us from evil in all its forms.

3. Titles for Jesus

- **Rabbi** was the title or address given by a student to his *Teacher* of the Law (cf. 'The Teacher' also in this story). The fact that Jesus is addressed by his disciples and those outside his immediate circle as Rabbi, probably indicates some uncertainly about both his identity and his mission. People treated him as the only kind of religious leader which they knew.

- **Lord** is used by Martha several time in addressing Jesus (Lord, from the Greek, *Kyrios*). It was a word which indicated power and authority. Its use here and in the other three gospels shows the faith of the early Christian communities from which the Gospels come. They recognized 'Jesus as Lord', i.e. the Saviour, the one whom God raised from the dead *(Romans 10:9)*. As the word *Lord* was used for God in the Old Testament, there can be no doubt that the faith of the early Church recognized the power and presence of God in Jesus, in his words and actions.

personal reflection

(between group sessions)

Make your own personal statement of faith in Jesus.

Clue: Martha says to Jesus, "Yes, Lord, I believe that you are the Christ, the Son of God, he who is coming into the world."

something to think about

...

A Prayer to the Pain of Jesus

Father,
when crutches were thrown away
did your Son limp
after the running cripples?

Did Jesus' eyes dim
when Bartimaeus saw?
Did life ebb in him
when it flowed in Lazarus?

When lepers leapt in new flesh
did scales appear
on the back of his hand?
The gospels say

Jesus felt power go out from him
but neglect to say
whether at that moment
pain came in.

Did the Son of God
take on ungrown legs and dead eyes
in the terrifying knowledge
that pain does not go away,
only moves on?

(John Shea, **The Hour of the Unexpected**, Argus Communications, 1979)

The Feeding of the Five Thousand

$\blacksquare$ $\blacksquare$ $\blacksquare$ $\blacksquare$ $\blacksquare$ $\blacksquare$ $\blacksquare$ $\blacksquare$ $\blacksquare$ $\blacksquare$ $\blacksquare$ $\blacksquare$

The apostles returned to Jesus, and told him all that they had done and taught. And he said to them, "Come away by yourselves to a lonely place and rest a while." For many were coming and going, and they had no leisure even to eat. And they went away in the boat to a lonely place by themselves.

Now many saw them going, and knew them, and they ran there on foot from all the towns, and got there ahead of them. As he went ashore he saw a great throng, and he had compassion on them, because they were like sheep without a shepherd; and he began to teach them many things. And when it grew late, his disciples came to him and said, "This is a lonely place, and the hour is now late; send them away, to go into the country and villages round about and buy themselves something to eat." But he answered them, "You give them something to eat." And they said to him, "Shall we go and buy two hundred denarii-worth of bread, and give it to them to eat?" And he said to them, "How many loaves have you? Go and see." And when they had found out, they said, "Five, and two fish."

Then he commanded them all to sit down by companies upon the green grass. So they sat down in groups, by hundreds and by fifties. And taking the five loaves and the two fish, he looked up to heaven, and blessed, and broke the loaves, and gave them to the disciples to set before the people; and he divided the two fish among them all. And they all ate and were satisfied. And they took up twelve baskets full of broken pieces and of the fish. And those who ate the loaves were five thousand men.

(Mark 6:30-44)

reflection • questions

1. Who are the characters in this story?

2. What kinds of relationships can you see?
Between whom?
(e.g. Jesus and the crowd)

3. Where is God in this story?

4. a) Can you see in what ways this is a Eucharistic story?
b) If we had **only** this Eucharistic story,
what could we say about the Eucharist?

5. What other stories does this story remind you of?
Why?
(cf. Clusters p. 18)

1. Compassion and Eucharist

We usually think of the word *compassion* as meaning pity, or being sorry for someone. We may even understand it as stronger than that – suffering with. When the Word of God took flesh, he entered into human suffering and broken-ness. The Hebrew word for compassion *rachamim*, refers in fact to the womb of Yahweh. The Greek verb *splangchnizomai* is about the entrails of the body, the guts. When we hear that Jesus had compassion on the crowds, 'because they were like sheep without a shepherd', it means that he was moved totally from within the centre of his being, to suffer with the people, to enter into their pain in order to do something about it. The implications of being compassionate run very deep. When we celebrate Eucharist, it is the compassionate Jesus who feeds us with himself – how can we then not have compassion on those without food – physical and spiritual? Accepting being feed means we have to feed others.
John Shea, the American theologian, tells the story of a man in Chicago who gave away free sandwiches to people in the dole queue beside his baker's shop. When he was asked why, the man said that in the great Depression of the 1930s, when he was starving, someone gave him sandwiches which actually saved his life. "If you get sandwiches," said the man, "you gotta give sandwiches."

■ Notice in this story that Jesus gives his disciples the responsibility of feeding the people. Two hundred denarii was a lot of money – a labourer's wages for a day was one denarius. Try to put that in modern currency! The disciples were aware only of the difficulty, indeed the impossibility of the task. Jesus, on the other hand, used the resources to hand, what was already there to be used.

2. Numbers

We need not take literally any of the numbers (for example, 5,000 or 5 loaves and 2 fish) but remember it is full of metaphors, which are intended to remind listeners that in the desert (the lonely place) Jesus feeds people, just as his Father fed the Israelites with manna during the desert wanderings (cf. Temptations p. 23). The Son is the image of the Father in word and deed. We can recall, too, the story of Elijah and the angel in the wilderness *(1 Kings 19:4-8)*: "And he arose, and ate and drank, and went in the strength of that food forty days and forty nights to Horeb the mountain of God."

The twelve baskets of the story remind us Christians of the twelve apostles. The number 12 was significant to the people of Israel because they were divided into twelve tribes – the descendants of Jacob *(cf. Genesis 49:1-21)*: "All these are the twelve tribes of Israel and this is what their father (Jacob) said to them as he blessed them ..."

personal reflection

(between group sessions)

Am I conscious of wanting to be fed by Jesus?

Am I ready to take responsibility for feeding others?

something to think about

...

The Song of the Bread

Bread from seed sown in earth
bread made by human hands
bread tasting of sorrow
and of men of many lands

bread of war and of peace
unchanging daily bread
strange bread of affection
and the stone bread of the dead

bread, our body our all
earned with such bitter sweat
bread, life with our fellows
whom we easily forget

bread without which we die
matter of such great worth
bread shared with each other
throughout all our life on earth.

Bread of life shared with us –
you give yourself as food
you, man among others
and a God of flesh and blood.

(Huub Oosterhuis, **Your Word is Near**, *Newman Press*,
1968, pp. 121-122)

The Prodigal Son

■ ■ ■ ■ ■ ■ ■ ■ ■ ■ ■

Now the tax collectors and sinners were all drawing near to hear him. And the Pharisees and the scribes murmured, saying, "This man receives sinners and eats with them."

And he said, "There was a man who had two sons; and the younger of them said to his father, 'Father, give me the share of property that falls to me.' And he divided his living between them. Not many days later, the younger son gathered all he had and took his journey into a far country, and there he squandered his property in loose living. And when he had spent everything, a great famine arose in that country, and he began to be in want. So he went and joined himself to one of the citizens of that country, who sent him into his fields to feed swine. And he would gladly have fed on the pods that the swine ate; and no one gave him anything. But when he came to himself, he said, 'How many of my father's hired servants have bread enough and to spare, but I perish here with hunger! I will arise and go to my father, and I will say to him, 'Father, I have sinned against heaven and before you; I am no longer worthy to be called your son; treat me as one of your hired servants.' And he arose and came to his father. But while he was yet at a distance, his father saw him and had compassion, and ran and embraced him and kissed him. And the son said to him, "Father, I have sinned against heaven and before you; I am no longer worthy to be called your son." But the father said to his servants, "Bring quickly the best robe, and put it on him; and put a ring on his hand, and shoes on his feet; and bring the fatted calf and kill it, and let us eat and make merry; for this my son was dead, and is alive again; he was lost, and is found." And they began to make merry."

"Now his elder son was in the field; and as he came and drew near to the house, he heard music and dancing. And he called one of the servants and asked what this meant. And he said to him, "Your brother has come, and your father has killed the fatted calf, because he has received him safe and sound." But he was angry and refused to go in. His father came out and entreated him, but he answered his father, "Lo, these many years I have served you, and I have never disobeyed your command; yet you never gave me a kid, that I might make merry with my friends. But when this son of yours came, who has devoured your living with harlots, you killed for him the fatted calf!" And he said to him, "Son, you are always with me, and all that is mine is yours. It was fitting to make merry and be glad, for this your brother was dead, and is alive; he was lost, and is found."

(*Luke 15:1,2,11-32*)

reflection • questions

1. For groups: After initial responses to the story, the group leader asks all the people in the group:
With whom do you identify in this story?

2. After this has been shared – the total group is divided into threes. In these groups, each member of the group becomes one of the characters:
  • father
  • elder son
  • younger son.
Each tells the story in her/his own words, from the point of view of the character she or he has chosen.
(*If the group is more easily divided by four, ask for an observer in each small group. An observer listens as each member tells the story, but makes no comment. In the general sharing afterwards the observer may comment on what went on in the group, noting the feelings, emotions, perhaps new insights gained, though not in a critical way.*)

3. Each member of the groups of three, is then invited to share with the larger group:
  a) how it felt to be his/her particular character
  b) how it felt to listen to the story as told by the other characters.

4. Continuing in the total group – the group leader asks people to reflect on the following:
  • Eating is mentioned three times in this story:
    a) Why do you think this is significant?
    b) Does this story raise a question about who you eat with? Or refuse to eat with?
  • What other title could this story have?

1. Levels of story

The background to the story of the Prodigal Son can be found in the Jewish inheritance of Jesus. We see in the gospels that he was very familiar with the Hebrew scriptures (what we now call the Old Testament). He frequently quoted the scriptures *(e.g. Deuteronomy 8:3, 6:16 and 6:13, in Matthew 4:1-11 – The Temptations)*.

The story of Joseph, Jacob's favourite son, was very well known to all religious Jews, and was significant in the story of the relationship between God and the people of Israel. Many of the metaphors and symbols in the story of the Prodigal Son come out of the Joseph story, though the parable is obviously not just a re-telling of that story. However, we need to be aware of:

- a family dispute
- a beloved son leaving home
- a far country (Egypt)
- famine
- return and the signs of welcome and status: the fatted calf,

the best robe, the shoes and the ring.

2. What is a parable?

Parables are stories characteristically associated with Jesus. He followed in the tradition of the rabbis who taught their disciples by means of stories – stories are easy to remember. Jesus used situations, people, events with which his audience was familiar:

- sowing seeds
- looking after sheep
- buying and selling

and in this parable, the family row which everyone knows about.

But parables are not just little moral tales or fables. Jesus meant to shock his listeners. His parables did not end as the hearers would expect, e.g. in this parable, we simply do not know if the elder son ever forgives the younger. Because the parable does not end as we expect, it shatters our assumptions, and becomes a call to action – a call to change and conversion. This is about changing our image of God, of Jesus and of self.

Many parables may ask us to look again at our images of God *(e.g. the labourers in the vineyard, Matthew 20)*. When we hear and reflect upon the parables of Jesus today, we are experiencing his invitation to change our attitudes and behaviour. The parables teach us about ourselves. J D Crossen says of parable, "I'm not sure what it's saying, but I am sure I don't like it!" Parables are not for our comfort.

personal reflection

(between group sessions)

Is there someone in the family,
in the neighbourhood,
at work,
whom you have not forgiven?

something to think about

...

The Prodigal Son

He is far off, he is very far off, he's blur
Of shadow against the setting sun, he is ragged
Clearly and slow and there is a touch of shame
And even penitence. In his vineyards his father
Is gazing at the crop, the promising early
Fruits but suddenly for no apparent reason
He lifts his torso, tilts his head and shades
His eye and something very familiar, a gesture
Of a child who has misbehaved is silhouetted
Against the bonfire blaze, "It is my son at last, at last it is
My dear lost son, my promising one, the part
Of my heart I've missed for nearly a dozen years."
In the kitchen a clatter of dishes proceeds and good
Herby smells rise up but the father is running
Fleet as a boy again and the shadow too turns
In an old and hopeless way. The boy doesn't move
For he is still a boy to his father. The sky
Is festive pink and purple. The father throws arms
About the boy and kisses the thin pinched face,
Smells the dirty clothes and a godlike but also extremely
Human compassion is seen against the light
And the boy is crying babyishly but now
Treading slowly the old good road to home
Through olive trees and herbs and the starting grapes
But in the house someone is slamming doors
And swearing and saying "It isn't fair. I was good"

and the prodigal is afraid till his father goes
And coaxes the elder son to the gala meal,
And grapes it seems have been burst across the sky.
Wine is running along the slopes of night
As a household starts to heal.

(Elizabeth Jennings, *Tributes*, Carcanet, 1989)

Labourers in the Vineyard

■ ■ ■ ■ ■ ■ ■ ■ ■ ■ ■ ■

Jesus said, "For the kingdom of heaven is like a house-holder who went out early in the morning to hire labourers for his vineyard. After agreeing with the labourers for a denarius a day, he sent them into his vineyard. And going out about the third hour he saw others standing idle in the market place; and to them he said, 'You go into the vineyard too, and whatever is right I will give you.' So they went. Going out again about the sixth hour and the ninth hour, he did the same. And about the eleventh hour he went out and found others standing; and he said to them, 'Why do you stand here idle all day?' They said to him, 'Because no one has hired us.' He said to them, 'You go into the vineyard too.' And when evening came, the owner of the vineyard said to his steward, 'Call the labourers and pay them their wages, beginning with the last, up to the first.' And when those hired about the eleventh hour came, each of them received a denarius. Now when the first came, they thought they would receive more; but each of them also received a denarius. And on receiving it they grumbled at the householder, saying 'These last worked only one hour, and you have made them equal to us who have borne the burden of the day and the scorching heat.' But he replied to one of them, 'Friend, I am doing you no wrong; did you not agree with me for a denarius? Take what belongs to you and go; I choose to give to this last as I give to you. Am I not allowed to do what I choose with what belongs to me? Or do you begrudge my generosity?' So the last will be first, and the first last."

(Matthew 20:1-6)

reflection • questions

1. With whom do you identify
in the story?
Why?

2. Is there anything in the story
which make you feel
uncomfortable?
Why?

3. What picture of Jesus,
the storyteller,
emerges from this parable?

4. What images of God are there
in this story?

5. Where is the vineyard
in which you work?

6. In what ways does this story
help us as lay people,
religious and clergy
to reflect on our roles
in the Church
and in the world?

background

1. Read again 'What is a parable?'

(p. 72)

2. Jesus the Prophet

Jesus was a prophet, in the line of the great prophets of the Old Testament – Isaiah, Jeremiah, Elijah, who challenged the situations of their day. A prophet is someone who speaks for God, who speaks the truth because she/he sees what is wrong in a situation where others do not see it or choose to ignore it. The prophet is an uncomfortable person to have around because she/he calls people to change, to repent, to be converted to the true worship of God in their hearts, not in externals.

The prophets of the Old Testament were signs of contradiction, because they stood out in sharp contrast to the society of their time. The prophets saw the situation through the eyes of God – a God on the side of the powerless, not through the eyes of the powerful of this world *(e.g. Isaiah 58:4-9 and Amos 8:4-6)*. They spoke for justice and truth. The prophets called the people to remember the past, the Covenant God had made with them, to see the present situation in the light of that past so as to build a future where God's will would be done.

"In the imperial world of Pharaoh and Solomon the prophetic alternative is a bad joke either to be squelched by force or ignored in satiation. But we are a haunted people because we believe the bad joke is rooted in the character of God himself, a God who is not the reflection of Pharaoh or of Solomon. He is a God with a name of his own which cannot be uttered by anyone but him. He is not the reflection of any, for he has his own person and retains that all to himself. He is a God uncredentialed in the empire, unknown in the courts, unwelcome in the temple. and his history begins in his attentiveness to the cries of the marginal ones. He, unlike his royal regents, is one whose person is presented as passion and pathos, the power

to care, the capacity to weep, the energy to grieve and then to rejoice. The prophets after Moses know that his caring, weeping, grieving, and rejoicing will not be outflanked by royal hardware or royal immunity because this one is indeed God. And kings must face that."
(Walter Brueggemann, **The Prophetic Imagination,** Fortress Press, 1978, p. 42)

As Son of God, Jesus was most aware of what was wrong, and of the change of heart to which God was calling his people. The parables of Jesus are an essential part of his prophetic stance. He spoke God's truth whether people wanted to hear it or not. Doing this laid him open to the anger of powerful enemies (cf. The woman in the synagogue p. 34), and eventually led him to his death.

Jesus is truly the prophet, the Word of God, spoken in flesh. He is the embodiment of the living truth, and so actually being in himself the model, the image of the God of truth in whose name he came, and in whose name he spoke.

3. Sharers in Christ's mission

It is clear in the documents of the Second Vatican Council, and in the Apostolic Exhortation, *Christifideles laici* (1989) that all the baptised are called upon to be prophets because we are all 'Christed' and therefore share in the prophetic mission of Jesus. We are all given the light and power of the Holy Spirit in Baptism and Confirmation to see situations with God's eyes, to say 'This is not how things should be', and to work to change situations of injustice at home, at work, in the world of economics and politics, both in our own country and in the wider world. This is not a matter of choice. It is an imperative because of our call to be responsible for helping to make 'thy kingdom come'.

The laity share Christ's mission as Prophet-Teacher.

This gives them the capacity to believe the gospel and the responsibility to proclaim it with courage.

They come to appreciate the Church's faith that cannot err in matters of belief.

They are called to allow the Gospel's power to shine out in their everyday lives.

Despite all contemporary contradictions they must proclaim their hope of future glory. (See, *Christifideles laici*, section 14, Grail, 1989, p. 21).

4. The Vineyard

Israel was often referred to in the Old Testament as the Lord's vineyard, e.g. Psalm 80:9 ff.
"Thou didst bring a vine out of Egypt; thou didst drive out the nations and plant it...

...Look down from heaven and see; have regard for this vine, the stock which thy right hand has planted."

A key passage is found in Isaiah 5:1-7:

"Let me sing for my beloved a love song concerning his vineyard.
My beloved had a vineyard on a very fertile hill...
...For the vineyard of the Lord of hosts is the house of Israel."

(See also: Jeremiah 2:21; Ezekiel 15:1; Hosea 10:1)

The strength of the metaphor of the vineyard was, therefore, fully appreciated among the Jews who heard Jesus. He used it in other teaching also: Matthew 21:33-46; Luke 13:6-9; John 15:1-6. However, it is not just Israel nor indeed the Church, but all of creation which is the Lord's vineyard.

5. *Parables and the Kingdom of God*

Some of the parables of Jesus refer directly to the 'kingdom of heaven' or 'the kingdom of God'. These are ways of referring to the change in people's hearts and behaviour if God's reign did indeed prevail. Jesus came to bring God's kingdom on earth – that was central to his mission, 'The time is fulfilled and the kingdom of God is at hand: repent and believe in the gospel' *(Mark 1:15).*

It is very tempting in the light of all this to think that these challenging stories were meant only for people who heard Jesus speak. We need to remember that they are for us, now, today, as individuals and as a community. We need always to ask ourselves: What questions is this story asking me, us, now?

The kingdom is not yet complete and we, as followers of Jesus, are given the responsibility of making it complete, visible on earth, by living our lives as witnesses to the gospel, taking our values from the Jesus story and not from this world's standards.

The parables show us how different are the standards of the kingdom to the standards of the world – and ask us to choose.

*Do I resent others
who come to work
in the same vineyard as myself?*

something to think about

...

"We've done our bit all these years"

"I've always worked hard in this parish – done my bit
since we moved here nearly 20 years ago. First it was
with the youth club and then the SVP and I'm still
very involved there – chairperson. My wife and I are
in the prayer group and we go to the bible study
group when we can. She's the secretary of the UCM.
Fr John, the last parish priest, always seemed glad of
the help and we were only delighted to give a hand.
When he introduced special ministers of the Eucharist, we felt so privileged to be chosen. That was
seven years ago at Christmas. Then last year we got a
new parish priest, Fr Michael, younger than Fr John
and very nice in his way. But he's got his own ideas,
if you know what I mean. He called a meeting of all
the Eucharistic ministers and said that maybe it was
time to have some new younger people involved.
We're to be de-commissioned, as it were, at the beginning of Lent, and new people appointed. Well, I
must say, I feel very let down, but he says that minis-
tries don't belong to us, that we only serve for a
while. He seems to want people who haven't really
done much to be involved – even some who have
just come back to the Church or even converts. I'm
sure it's all very well, but it doesn't seem as if he
really recognises all we've done. I hope I'm not being
proud, but I must say we do feel let down. After all,
we've done our bit all these years."

The Road to Emmaus

■ ■ ■ ■ ■ ■ ■ ■ ■ ■ ■

Session 1

That very day two of them were going to a village named Emmaus, about seven miles from Jeruslaem, and talking with each other about all these things that had happened. While they were talking and discussing together, Jesus himself drew near and went with them. But their eyes were kept from recognising him. and he said to them, "What is this conversation which you are holding with each other as you walk?" And they stood still, looking sad. Then one of them, named Cleopas, answered him, "Are you the only visitor to Jerusalem who does not know the things that have happened there in these days?" And he said to them, "What things?"

And they said to him, "Concerning Jesus of Nazareth, who was a prophet mighty in deed and word before God and all the people, and how our chief priests and rulers delivered him up to be condemned to death and crucified him. But we had hoped that he was the one to redeem Israel. Yes, and besides all this, it is now the third day since this happened. Moreover, some women of our company amazed us. They were at the tomb early in the morning and did not find his body; and they came back saying that they had even seen a vision of angels, who said that he was alive. Some of those who were with us went to the tomb, and found it just as the women had said; but him they did not see."

And he said to them, "O foolish men, and slow of heart to believe all that the prophets have spoken! Was it not necessary that the Christ should suffer these things and enter into his glory?" And beginning with Moses and all the prophets, he interpreted to them in all the scriptures the things concerning himself.

So they drew near to the village to which they were going. He appeared to be going further, but they constrained him, saying, "Stay with us, for it is towards evening and the day is now far spent." So he went in to stay with them. When he was at table with them, he took the bread and blessed, and broke it, and gave it to them. And their eyes were opened and they recognised him; and he vanished out of their sight. They said to each other, "Did not our hearts burn within us while he talked to us on the road, while he opened to us the scriptures?"

And they rose that same hour and returned to Jerusalem; and they found the eleven gathered together and those who were with them, who said, "The Lord has risen indeed, and has appeared to Simon!" Then they told what had happened on the road, and how he was known to them in the breaking of the bread.
(Luke 24 : 13 - 35)

reflection • questions

1. What do we learn from this story about
   a) the attitude of these two disciples
      • toward Jesus?
      • towards the possibility
        of his resurrection?
   b) the attitude of the group of
      disciples in Jerusalem
      • towards Jesus?
      • towards the possibility
        of his resurrection?
   c) Why do these attitudes change?

2. From this story, what do we learn about what is involved in being a disciple of Jesus?

3. Can you see in this story any stages of a journey?

4. Does this story remind you of any other journey stories, in the Bible or outside it? Name them.
In what ways are they are similar?

5. In what ways do you think this story is a metaphor?
(cf. Metaphors and symbols p.22)

6. Has this story anything to say to your own story of journeying in faith?

1. Four moments

- In any Bible story, there are four essential stages or moments:
  - movement
  - danger
  - hope
  - new beginnings

- Above all, these are clear in journey stories, cf. Abraham, Jacob, Moses, Elijah, Jesus, his disciples. When we reflect on Bible stories, we can be helped to see these moments in our own jourey. Because we are a people of hope, following Jesus through his death and resurrection – and our own – there is always the possibility of a new beginning. The God of journeys at the same time both goes ahead of us and walks with us. This Emmaus story is not just about the events of an afternoon's walk, but is a metaphor for a lifetime's journey. A metaphor is at once true and not true in the literal sense (See p. 22). It is a way of expressing the inexpressible, describing the indescribable, in familar words and experiences. At best, our words for the most significant experiences of life; falling in love, giving birth, being bereaved, are halting and inadequate. We use what we know to express what has happened to us. The metaphor of journey (of moving, or being moved to another place) is used to describe or express a change in our lives, and in their direction. After this journey, these two disciples were never the same again – their whole life's journey is encapsulated in this one walk. The outward journey is the metaphor for an inward journey towards recognition and change of heart, a conversion, turning around. "Did not our hearts burn within us as he talked to us on the road, as he opened to us the scriptures?" *(Luke 24:32)*

2. Journey stories

Journey stories are one of the most important kinds or types of story in the Bible, both Old and New Testaments. The great stories of the Old Testament, e.g. Abraham, Jacob, Joseph, the Exodus and the Exile are all concerned with journeys and journeying. Likewise, in the New Testament, we find many examples: the Flight into Egypt, the Prodigal Son, all the travels and preaching of Jesus, and, above all, his journey towards Jerusalem, which is of tremendous significance in Luke's gospel. It begins in Luke 9:51, 'When the days drew near for him to be received up, he set his face to go to Jeruslaem' – to Jerusalem, where he would die, for this journey was to end, apparently, in his death.

3. Discipleship – above all Jesus is <u>the</u> disciple, the way to the Father

Discipleship is about freely putting oneself on the same road as the Master, following in his way. It is to do with answering a call, and involves, above all, a personal attachment to Christ. It is more than an invitation to believe in a set of doctrines. To be a disciple is to believe in and love a person. Being a disciple of Jesus means taking on his way of life, while recognising that to live as Jesus lived inevitably involves death – taking up his cross and following him.

personal reflection

(between group sessions)

*Recall a moment when your heart
'burned within you',
e.g. a book you read,
something someone said,
a sight that moved you.
Allow yourself to relive its joy
and pain,
and talk to God about it
in your own way.*

something to think about

...

Now the green blade riseth from the buried grain,
wheat that in the dark earth many days has lain;
Love lives again, that with the dead has been;
love is come again like wheat that springeth green.

In the grave they laid him, love whom men had slain,
thinking that never he would wake again,
laid in the earth like grain that sleeps unseen:
love is come again like wheat that springeth green.

Forth he came at Easter, like the risen grain,
he that for three days in the grave had lain;
quick from the dead my risen Lord is seen:
love is come again like wheat that springeth green.

When our hearts are wintry, grieving or in pain,
thy touch can call us back to life again;
fields of our heart that dead and bare have been:
love is come again like wheat that springeth green.

(JMC Crum, *The Oxford Book of Carols*, OUP)

The Road to Emmaus

Session 2

(Text as on page 81)

reflection • questions

1. Personal reflection:
   a) What can you recall from the last session of reflecting on this story, e.g. what was said about Jesus? journey? discipleship?
   b) How did this touch your own story?

2. Reread the Feeding of the Five Thousand *(Mark 6:30-44)*.
   What do these two stories have in common?
   Of what other Old Testament or New Testament stories do they remind you? Why?

3. What do we learn from these stories
   • about God?
   • about Jesus?

4. What in the Emmaus story reminds you of the Eucharist/Mass?

5. Why do you think 'he was known to them in the breaking of the bread'?
   How did they recognise him?

1. God takes us where, who and as we are

The two disciples are confused, sad, perhaps even running away, broken by their disappointment, and Jesus comes and walks with them and changes them. Many of the great figures of the Bible do not seem, at first sight, to be the most likely characters for God's choice to fall upon – but when we look at

- Jacob, the cheat
- Moses, the Coward
- David, the Adulterer

we see that God can make something of the most unpromising material. We see, in the New Testament, Jesus does the same thing: a tax collector, Levi, becomes one of the chosen twelve; the Samaritan woman is sent to bring the good news to her fellow citizens; Peter, who denies him, becomes the leader of the apostles. God's concern is never limited to what we are, but much more to what we may become.

2. A typical gesture

The two disciples recognised Jesus in the breaking of the bread. This was a gesture typical fo him, by which he was easily recognisable. They had obviously been with him on other occasions when he had taken bread, blessed, broken it and given it out to be shared. This is the gesture that sums up the whole life and death of Jesus – the bread, blessed, broken, shared is the symbol of his giving of himself to be broken, poured out and shared. Those who witnessed his death, understood what he meant when, at the Last Supper, he said, "Take: this is my body" and "This is my blood of the covenant which is poured out for many" *(Mark 14:22-24).*

3. The Eucharist

There are seven moments or movements in the Mass, which are clearly reflected in the structure of the Emmaus story:

Mass/Eucharist

1. Gathering of the community, as we are, bringing our own stories and lives with us, aware of our failings.

2. We tell God the story of our concerns, sad or joyful, collected by the priest in the Opening Prayer.

3. We listen to the Word, in the readings and in the homily.

4. Procession of the gifts of bread and wine – symbols of what we are, and have.

5. Eucharistic Prayer.

6. The Communion Rite – the Sign of Peace, Breaking of bread, Eucharist shared.

7. The Dismissal. "Go in peace to love and serve the Lord" – we are sent out.

Emmaus Story

1. Jesus meets the two disciples on the road – as they are.

2. Jesus encourages them to tell their story, their concerns.

3. Jesus tells them of himself – he opens the scriptures to them.

4. Jesus takes the bread, the symbol of life shared.

5. Jesus blesses the bread.

6. Jesus breaks the bread, and gives it to them.

7. The disciples immediately go back to tell the good news.

4. Stories are never finished.

"A story is more like an onion than a peach." *(Rev T Hamill)*

Approaching this story of the road to Emmaus in two different ways, helps us to understand that every Bible story has many layers and levels of meaning, and that we can never exhaust these. To say, 'The meaning of this story is..' is to undervalue the power of the story, to strip it of its significance. Each time it is told or read, the story is different: depending on the situation in which we hear it, a different meaning can be discerned. The story has the power to touch us, in our many different circumstances, because God, who is present in the story, can touch us as we are, if we allow him and the story to speak to us.

What is my typical gesture?

something to think about

...

Father, all-powerful and ever-living God,
we do well always and everywhere to give you thanks
through Jesus Christ our Lord.
At the last supper,
as he sat at table with his apostles,
he offered himself to you as the spotless lamb,
the acceptable gift that gives you perfect praise.
Christ has given us this memorial of his passion,
to bring us its saving power until the end of time.

In this great sacrament you feed your people
and strengthen them in holiness,
so that the family of mankind
may come to walk in the light of one faith,
in one communion of love.
We come then to this wonderful sacrament
to be fed at your table
and grow into the likeness of the risen Christ.
Earth unites with heaven
to sing the new song of creation
as we adore and praise you for ever.

(Preface of The Holy Eucharist II, Weekday Missal)

3

Looking at our own stories

*T*his session may be fitted into the group meetings at any time, when the members feel that, by sharing deeply and personally, they have established sufficient trust and ease. Because it is so personal, it must be handled with great care! The gospel story comes at the end, so the order of the session is different from the others.

1. Group members read Section 4 'What do we mean by Story?' (p. 9)

They are then invited, by the leader, to share anything which strikes them, with the total group (15 mins).

2. Members then need 10 minutes personal reading and reflection on the following questions:

   i   Can you see any similarities between the writer's story and your own? In what ways?

   ii Can you name any of the important strands in your own life-story?

   iii What have been some of the most significant experiences in your life?

   iv Who have been some of the most important people in your life?

   v   Can you name an important decision which you have made? Or refused to make?

   vi What gifts have you been given for which you are grateful?

vii What wounds or hurts have you suffered:

- in your personal life?
- in your professional life?
- in your family life?
- in your life in the Church?

3. Group members are then invited in small groups to share appropriately their answers to these questions. (30 mins)

4. In the total group, members are invited (but not pressurized!) to share one or two of their reflections on these questions (15 mins).

5. Group members are asked to think for a few moments, whether there is any gospel story which had and/or has significance for them at a particular moment in their lives. They are then invited to share this with the group and say why it is significant (10 mins).

6. Closing prayer. Group leader or member reads aloud **The finding in the temple** (Luke 2:41-52). (5 mins.)

Now his parents went to Jerusalem every year at the feast of the Passover. And when he was twelve years old, they went up according to custom; and when the feast was ended, as they were returning, the boy Jesus stayed behind in Jerusalem. His parents did not know it, but supposing him to be in the company they went a day's journey, and they sought him among their kinsfolk and acquaintances; and when they did not find him, they returned to Jerusalem, seeking him.

After three days they found him in the temple, sitting among the teachers, listening to them and asking them questions; and all who heard him were amazed at his understanding and his answers. And when they saw him they were astonished; and his mother said to him, "Son, why have you treated us so? Behold, your father and I have been looking for you anxiously." And he said to them"How is it that you sought me? Did you not know that I must be in my Father's house?" And they did not understand the saying which he spoke to them.

And he went down with them and came to Nazareth, and was obedient to them; and his mother kept all these things in her heart. And Jesus increased in wisdom and in stature, and in favour with God and man."

personal reflection

(between group sessions)

*Re-read the story of the **Finding in the Temple** by yourself. Does it say anything to your personal story?*

P A R T

4

Prayer Service for Walking the Road

*G*roups may wish to celebrate their time together with a short liturgy focussing on the word of God. This is probably best done at the last group meeting. What follows are only suggestions – the group can decide on its own form of liturgy, or have another kind of celebration,

Chairs should be arranged in a circle as usual, with either a large bible or the book of the gospels in a prominent position, on a stand or cushion, with candles and flowers to highlight it.

1. Opening hymn ... (O the word of my Lord , Hymns Old and New, 431)

2. Prayer:
Lord God of heaven and earth
you speak to us in your Word and in our lives.
In the name of Jesus Christ your Son,
and in the power of your Holy Spirit,
give us ears to hear you
eyes to see you
tongues to praise you
and hearts to love and serve you. Amen

3. Taize chant: In the Lord is my true salvation.

4. Reverencing the Bible /the Book of the Gospels

Group members are invited to come forward and reverence the Bible by some gesture or sign, e.g. a kiss, or making the sign of the cross on the book and on their own forehead or heart. This may be done in silence or to the accompaniment of meditative music.

5. Reading from the gospels: the group may choose any one of the gospel stories on which they have reflected together and read it aloud. Perhaps using two or three voices would make the reading more dramatic. This is followed by a few minutes personal reflection and a short time (5 to 10 minutes) sharing prayer/response about the gospel story.

6. The group is invited to recall any memorable moments during the sessions and thank God for these. (5 to 10 minutes).

7. Hymn ... (I will be with you, Hymns Old and New, 263)

8. Closing blessing recited together:
May the Lord bless us and keep us
May he make his face to shine upon us
May he look upon us with kindness
And give us his peace. Amen